COACHING FOR MANAGERS

BULLET GUIDE

Matt Somers

Hodder Education, 338 Euston Road, London NW1 3BH

Hodder Education is an Hachette UK company

First published in UK 2011 by Hodder Education

This edition published 2011

Copyright © 2011 Matt Somers

The moral rights of the author have been asserted

Database right Hodder Education (makers)

Artworks (internal and cover): Peter Lubach

Cover concept design: Two Associates

British Library Cataloguing in Publication Data: a catalogue record for this title is available from the British Library.

10 9 8 7 6 5 4 3 2 1

The publisher has used its best endeavours to ensure that any website addresses referred to in this book are correct and active at the time of going to press. However, the publisher and the author have no responsibility for the websites and can make no guarantee that a site will remain live or that the content will remain relevant, decent or appropriate.

The publisher has made every effort to mark as such all words which it believes to be trademarks. The publisher should also like to make it clear that the presence of a word in the book, whether marked or unmarked, in no way affects its legal status as a trademark.

Every reasonable effort has been made by the publisher to trace the copyright holders of material in this book. Any errors or omissions should be notified in writing to the publisher, who will endeavour to rectify the situation for any reprints and future editions.

Hachette UK's policy is to use papers that are natural, renewable and recyclable products and made from wood grown in sustainable forests. The logging and manufacturing processes are expected to conform to the environmental regulations of the country of origin.

www.hoddereducation.co.uk

Typeset by Stephen Rowling/Springworks

Printed in Spain

To my daughter Evie for… well, just for being you

About the author

Matt Somers is a coaching practitioner of many years' experience. He works with a host of clients in the North East of England, where his firm is based, and throughout the UK and beyond. His coaching skills training programmes have been attended by managers from a range of blue-chip organizations such as HSBC, Scottish & Southern Energy, Sage and Toyota.

Acknowledgements

I would like to thank Carol, Lesley and Leanne who have worked with me over the years to refine the ideas presented here. Similarly, working with Kris, Ashley, Lisa and, more recently, Katie has enabled me to see the modern world of work through younger, fresher eyes.

My good friend – and extraordinary trainer – Mike Butler provided the 'Mum and Dad' exercise in Chapter 7.

Matt Somers, Castle Eden, County Durham
May 2011

Contents

Introduction

If you're a manager of people in any way, you'll know the frustrations that come with the role. You have to allocate tasks and deal with the administration but you also have to **keep up morale and motivation** and make sure your team are performing **at the top of their game**.

No easy task, but made infinitely more straightforward – and enjoyable – when you know how to coach.

There are many formal definitions of coaching, but for our purposes we can consider it as simply **a way of communicating** with people that allows them to access their ability and do their best work. As we'll see, it is an approach that **raises awareness**, **generates responsibility** and **builds trust**. It requires us, as managers, to **ask more than tell** and be prepared to listen – **really listen**. It is a big challenge, but the need to meet the challenge is even bigger.

Armed with an ability to coach for results, you'll be able to tap into those abilities you know your people have but which they seem sometimes to leave behind on their way to work.

This book is designed to give you the **tools and techniques** to understand what holds your people back and the means to help them move forward.

There are many formal definitions of coaching... we can consider it as simply a way of communicating with people that allows them to access their ability and do their best work

1 Coaching to release potential

Turning potential into results

'We must get the best out of people!' cry managers everywhere as they struggle to **achieve more and more with less and less**.

The phrase suggests that **the best is already in people to begin with** and that we just need to manage people in a way that lets it out.

This is the essence of coaching.

Coaching is about helping people realize their potential and convert it into results

· ·

Coaching is about helping people **realize their potential** and **convert it into results**.

* The starting point for any coach is to consider whether people have the potential to make the changes necessary to improve.
* The view that we take has a **profound effect** on the chances of coaching proving successful.
* The coaching approach uncovers what prevents people from accessing their potential.

> **'Leadership is unlocking people's potential to become better.'**
> Bill Bradley

Finding the potential

How much of your team's potential shows up at work?

Take a moment to think about this. Perhaps you can put a percentage on it. However you see it, how do you know? In other words, what evidence do you have to back up your figure?

* Having asked this question of countless managers, I have yet to get an answer of 100 per cent or even close; most say in the region of 30 to 60 per cent.
* Many managers describe people achieving amazing things *outside* of work which they wish they would bring *to* work.
* It all suggests that people have **a lot more to offer** than our management style allows them to give.

None of this is provable, though. There is no scientific test or psychological profiling tool that quantifies potential.

We are left, as coaches, with a need to choose our point of view. We must decide whether we want to work on the assumption that our people do have the potential needed or work on the assumption that they don't.

An optimistic view – the 'positive philosophical choice' – offers more scope for improvement and brings about a productive self-fulfilling prophecy.

There is no scientific test or psychological profiling tool that quantifies potential

Turning potential into performance

The job of management is to **convert potential into performance**.

Improved performance at work can manifest itself in many ways:

* selling more
* spending less
* improving quality
* improving the customer experience
* delivering on time
* changing redundant processes and procedures
* working in a team.

As we've already discussed, there is always a gap between potential and performance. We've established that people are not performing to their potential and that there is an identifiable difference between what people *could* do and what they actually do.

6

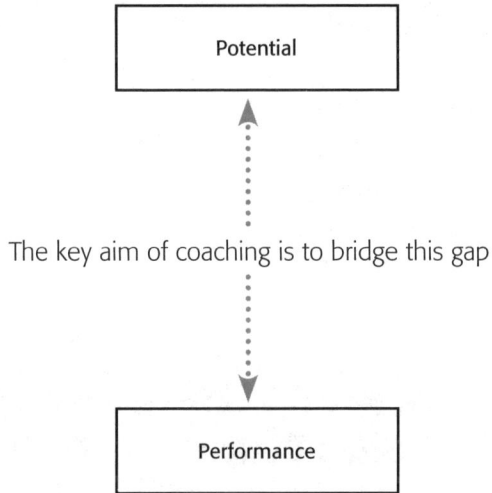

Figure 1.1: The gap between potential and performance

Bridging the gap

Orthodox training and development addresses the gap between potential and performance by seeking to add knowledge and skills. This is fine where the gap is to do with a lack of knowledge and skills.

If a PA, for example, is poor at managing their boss's diary because they don't know how to use the software, that's easily solved. They can go on a course or work through something online. If, however, they're poor at this task because they're bored, lack confidence, can't see the point or feel that it ought not be part of their role, it's a very different matter.

Where the performance issue is to do with willingness rather than ability... we must remove interference

Where the performance issue is to do with **willingness rather than ability**, the nature of the gap is different and so we need a different approach: we must remove interference.

For the purposes of thinking this through, I would suggest there are two kinds of interference:

1 **External** interference. This is the sort of interference that is going on around people at work as they try to perform their tasks.
2 **Internal** interference. This is the interference that people experience in their own heads – the thoughts and feelings that hold them back.

The things that interfere with potential

Here are some examples of both kinds of interference…

External:

* poor management
* poor relationships
* policy and procedures
* environment
* lack of time
* lack of budget.

Internal:

* trying too hard
* negative thoughts
* negative images
* negative beliefs
* limiting thoughts
* lack of self-trust
* a busy mind.

'Treat people as if they were what they ought to be and you help them to become what they are capable of being.'

Johann Wolfgang von Goethe

CASE STUDY: My first job

I once came across the original interview notes from my first job interview. The final line read: 'Mr Somers is worth taking on but only as a low achiever.'

I wonder if my first boss looked at that and thought, 'Well, if he's only a low achiever, we'd better just give him the simple, mundane jobs.'

This tendency to judge and label people often creates a self-fulfilling prophecy. Thankfully, I didn't see the note and didn't realize I was a 'low achiever' or I would surely have become one!

Coaching requires us to set aside any negative assumptions and work on the basis that people can realize their potential. This dramatically improves the chances that they will.

2 Coaching for motivation

The importance of motivation

* It is very difficult to coach people who don't want to be coached.
* Of course, it's difficult to get people to do anything at work if they don't really want to!
* Motivation is one of the **most important components** to get right when managing people.
* Alongside coaching people to reduce interference we need to ensure they are motivated to do so.

Motivation is one of the most important components to get right when managing people

● ●

* For the longest time, fear was the main motivation tool, from the whipping of slaves to the beating of stable boys.
* Unfortunately, fear is still a popular motivator, especially in tricky economic times. There is also an increase in the amount of workplace bullying being reported.
* More recently variations of the carrot and stick have been used.
* Salary increases, big bonuses, status symbols and the like are dangled as carrots.
* Declining bonuses, withholding promotions and risking being stuck in the same job for ever are used as sticks.

Motivation at work

Perhaps we need tools more sophisticated than those we use to motivate donkeys. Perhaps the motivational tools that were developed for the hard labour of industrial times no longer work. Perhaps the things that motivated people to do the simple, repetitive jobs of old don't work for the complex, creative jobs of today.

Consider this list of 'motivators':

Money, Incentives, Status, The cause, Holidays, Bonuses, A worthwhile job, Self-esteem, Pride, Self-actualization, Achievement, Fun, Getting better, Self-development, Socializing, Praise, Career prospects, Recognition, Belonging, Safety, Security.

What do you notice?

And if we separate them into two columns, what do you notice about them now?

* Money
* Incentives
* Status
* The cause
* Holidays
* Bonuses
* Socializing
* Praise
* Career prospects
* Recognition
* Belonging
* Safety
* Security

* A worthwhile job
* Self-esteem
* Pride
* Self-actualization
* Achievement
* Fun
* Getting better
* Self-development

Intrinsic motivation

The left-hand column on the previous page contains external (or extrinsic) motivators. They need to be **supplied by somebody else**. Without them there is no motivation but by themselves they are not enough to really motivate people.

We also need the internal (or intrinsic) motivators listed in the right-hand column. These keep people motivated over a much longer time frame and are more readily influenced by individual managers.

This is not to say that external motivation is not important or useful. It is but it only takes us so far. It might produce a climate we could think of as 'not demotivated'. It may well be all that's needed to get the job done, but to get the job done well requires people to be truly motivated and this means internal motivation, too.

18

The various internal motivators can be summarized and arranged on a triangle. The triangle shape is important as it conveys the balance and equality that we've established as being important.

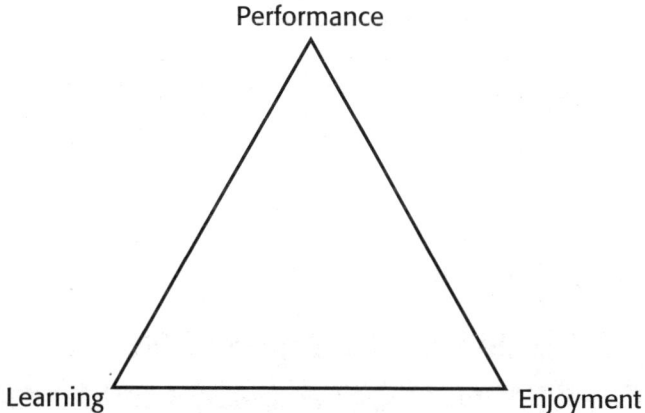

Figure 2.1: The three key internal motivators

Performance, learning and enjoyment

* **Performance** is about the motivation that comes from the prospect of **doing a job and doing it well**; drawing on people's potential and letting them play to their strengths.
* **Learning** is about much more than training and qualifications; it's about giving people work that is **interesting and varied**.
* **Enjoyment** is about providing work that is **intrinsically enjoyable**, not just arranging team nights out.

However, if we focus on any one of these key sources of internal motivation at the expense of the other two, there will always be problems sooner or later.

'True motivation comes from achievement, personal development, job satisfaction, and recognition.'

Frederick Herzberg

20

In the typical place of work, performance will be focused on the most. Rarely will executives emerge from the latest high-powered review meeting and announce that more enjoyment is needed and that enjoyment targets will be set in the coming weeks!

This is understandable given the short-term goals and targets which dominate our working lives.

Unfortunately, if the stress on the need to perform is so high that learning and enjoyment disappear, then ironically the chances of high performance are actually lessened.

It would be the same if learning and enjoyment were over stressed, too. Any one of the three components can be placed at the top of the triangle but we always need the other two.

Striking a balance

To understand this further, **consider the following examples**:

* too much studying without an opportunity to act on what we've learnt becomes frustrating and **learning suffers**
* too much enjoyment becomes boring after a while and **we don't enjoy our time as much**
* too high a focus on performance lessens the chance to learn and enjoy, which makes **sustaining high levels of performance more difficult**.

22

CASE STUDY: Work can be fun

One of our client organizations required its production line employees to spot faulty parts. This was not being done well and targets were being missed.

The management's response was effectively 'Do better, or else' (performance).

However, in an effort to implement the other elements of internal motivation, our client arranged quality circles to discuss how improvements to the fault-finding process could be achieved (learning) and also a competition for finding faulty parts with fun prizes for the winners (enjoyment).

As a result, motivation and consequently performance improved.

3 Coaching to raise awareness

The need to be aware

Coaching people is about helping them to **make a change**.

* Whether it's about solving a problem or improving a strength, there will always be a change to be made.
* However, before we can change anything we need to **become aware of how it is now**.
* We can only exert a measure of control over the things of which we are aware.
* Raising awareness is one of three key principles of effective coaching.

> **Before we can change anything we need to become aware of how it is now**

We might define awareness as:

'High quality focus and attention without judgement.'

A bathroom mirror gives us information that is useful if we want to shave or do our hair effectively, but it never offers any opinion or advice about shaving or hair styling. When coaching people we need to be similarly detached while helping people to become aware of what they need to change.

Questions to raise awareness

When coaching to raise awareness…

Do:

✔ *Use questions that make people think*
✔ *Let people describe what they notice*

Don't:

✘ *Give instructions that leave them with no need to think*
✘ *Dictate what people should notice*

Now **consider** the following scenario:

A manager is coaching a member of an enquiry team in a call centre. It's a very busy day and the monitoring system is showing quite lengthy call waiting times.

The manager is concerned that the teams should be empathetic with customers. Here's a couple of things she could say:

28

Which creates more awareness?

'Trying fails, awareness cures.'

Fritz Perls

Directing awareness

The first example is an instruction. It creates little, if any, awareness. It offers no clues as to how the employee might become more empathetic.

The second example is an awareness-raising coaching question. In order to answer it, the employee will be listening carefully to the customer's tone of voice, their volume, their speed of speaking and the language they use. This will give the employee insight into how they can communicate in a way that is much more on the customer's wavelength. In other words, they will be communicating with more empathy.

We must make sure our coaching encourages people to become more aware of things that are useful to them. As with the empathy example, we must coach people to become more aware of the qualities they would like to bring to the task at hand.

> *I've become aware that I'm really much more nervous than I realized.*

> *I've become aware that my customer is sitting forward and seeming a lot more interested.*

Encouraging **awareness towards things that are useful to people** is known as creating focus.

Getting clear on focus

* Focus is not the same as **'trying really hard'**.
* Trying and effort just lead to stress and exhaustion.
* Effort is overrated – what we should really value is results.

Unfortunately, we live in a world that prizes effort. We love our heroic failures and can be quite dismissive of people who can achieve results easily: 'Of course, Sally finds it easy to talk in public, she does amateur dramatics. It's all right for her but I have to really try hard to overcome my nerves.'

Focus needs to be **appropriate**.

We would coach a salesperson, for example, to focus on:

* the customer's tone
* the customer's body language
* keeping upbeat
* identifying what the customer needs

…and not to focus on:

* feeling nervous
* gaps in their product knowledge
* feeling tired
* worrying about losing the sale.

Awareness cures

Focus follows **interest** – and people's awareness and focus is governed by what they find curious and interesting.

Imagine I'm chairing a meeting and my biggest concern is that everybody contributes. I don't want to be coached on getting the agenda items in the right order and if you try to coach me on that it will be difficult for me to focus and concentrate.

Of course, this might mean we have to have a conversation about priorities, but that's a conversation we should probably have anyway.

CASE STUDY: Actually, you can do better

I was doing some coaching with a group of people who wanted to become better at public speaking. One person received some feedback which revealed they said the word 'actually' repeatedly. (At one point, they said: 'You can actually take the actual file and actually place it on the actual desktop.')

The person concerned said they would try really hard to stop, but my advice was that this was the last thing they should do. Instead I suggested they simply count how often they said 'actually' the next time they gave a talk.

Of course, becoming aware enough to be able to count meant they were aware enough to be able to stop and the problem simply disappeared.

4 Coaching to generate responsibility

The need for responsibility

* When we coach people we must recognize that, in the final analysis, it is only **they themselves who can make a change**.
* The old saying 'you can lead a horse to water, but you cannot make it drink' holds true.
* We need people to feel **empowered** and work well without constant supervision.
* Too many managers are exhausted by having to do far too many tasks that, in truth, the team could take on.
* Generating responsibility is another of the three key principles of effective coaching.

Too many managers are exhausted by having to do far too many tasks that, in truth, the team could take on

We might define responsibility as:

'A person's choice to own a task and see it through.'

* **Choice** means the person could have selected another option, but has elected instead to do what needs doing.
* **Ownership** means that the person sees the task and accountability for a successful outcome as theirs, not yours.

These days the word responsibility has some negative connotations at work. It has become synonymous with having piles more work to do. But in coaching the sound of the word gives us a big clue: *response-ability*.

Communication choices

How can we communicate in a more empowering way?

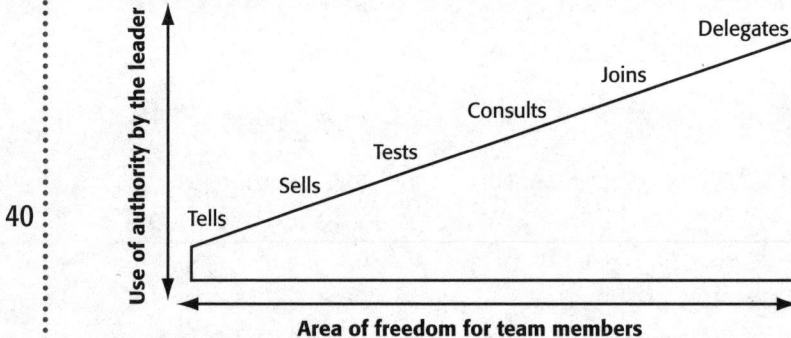

Figure 4.1: The different communication styles available to a leader

This well-known diagram illustrates that there are different communication styles depending on whether the leader exerts more or less of their authority.

How do we make the right communication choice?

Do:

✔ Consider the urgency of the task
✔ Consider the needs of the person with whom you're communicating
✔ Consider your own personality and style

Don't:

✘ Stick to one style rigidly
✘ Swing wildly from one style to another
✘ Adopt a style that simply isn't you

Telling really only works in crisis-type situations. Where quality of work or learning from the experience is most important, then telling is of little use and we need a much more exploratory, coaching style of communication.

Coaching and communication

Coaching solves many communication problems.

* The problem with the choices outlined earlier is that either the manager has control or the employee has control.
* Coaching means that both have control.
* The employee has control because they are choosing the way forward.
* The manager has control because they know exactly what is going to be done.
* The manager can check the intended action against procedures but does not have to check that the work is being carried out.

42

Coaching has many advantages:

* employees feel more involved
* employees respond to having their views valued
* more ideas are generated
* quality improves as employees feel the outcome is theirs
* while initially this approach takes longer, it quickly frees the manager for other tasks
* learning from experience is greatly enhanced.

'It is the responsibility of leadership to provide opportunity, and the responsibility of individuals to contribute.'

William Pollard

The problem with telling

Telling, on the other hand, has many disadvantages:

* you have to know how you get results yourself
* you have to find a way to get these ideas into another person's head
* it assumes one best way to get things done
* there is little chance of breakthroughs or innovation
* a relationship of dependence is established
* people can't remember what they were told.

44

> **'People think responsibility is hard to bear.
> It's not. I think that sometimes it is the absence
> of responsibility that is harder to bear.'**
>
> Henry Kissinger

Managers shy away from giving responsibility for **fear that things will go wrong**, but:

1 people cannot learn and improve without making mistakes
2 people are not 'getting it wrong' – they are learning
3 the higher the fear of making a mistake, the greater the chance of making a mistake
4 coaching can predict what mistakes could be made and develop plans for handling them.

The power of choice

Now imagine I say to you:

> *Please go and get sandwiches and coffees for these clients.*

On discovering the sandwich bar was closed, you'd be likely to come back to me and explain that this meant you couldn't do it.

Then, imagine I say to you:

> *Would you be willing to organize some lunch for these clients?*

This time you'd be more likely to do much more in trying to complete the task.

The difference is that in the second instance you are choosing to do it rather than feeling you have to do it. It's an important difference.

CASE STUDY: Choice and ownership

Sensing some tiredness at the end of a two-day coaching skills training programme, I worried that some participants wouldn't fully engage with the final practice session. In setting up the exercise, I decided to say:

'I realize that some of you are tired and might prefer to just have a chat. That would be a shame because this is your last opportunity to practise before you return to work. I want you to write down in your course manual what you intend to do with the next hour. You can decide you want to learn and practise some more or you can choose to rest. It's entirely up to you and I don't want to see what you've written, but make a choice and stick to it.'

This gave people choice and ownership (responsibility) and perhaps unsurprisingly everybody decided to put their energies into the exercise.

5 Coaching to build trust

The need for trust

Trust at work has never been more vital but seldom been scarcer.

* The big picture is not good as in modern times we have witnessed a wave of corporate scandals and tales of corruption.
* At a more detailed level a relationship of trust between manager and team member is absolutely essential to a productive working relationship.
* This is never truer than when seeking to utilize the benefits of coaching. The success of coaching directly correlates with the **amount of trust between coach and coachee**.

The success of coaching directly correlates with the amount of trust between coach and coachee

We might define trust as:

'A readiness to communicate without fear of consequences.'

* The people we coach need to know that what they tell us will be handled sensitively and, where appropriate, in confidence.
* The people we coach need to know that expressing difficulty will not be held against them in the future.
* Trust is another of the three key principles of effective coaching.

Who to trust?

Trust in oneself

* One of the main reasons why we coach others is to help them develop their self-belief.
* The highest performers in any field have **high levels of self-belief**.
* Belief is based on evidence so it is vital our coaching enables people to achieve successes, however small to begin with.
* It follows that they must know they themselves were responsible for the success.

Trust in the coach

* It is vitally important that the people we coach trust us to do so professionally.
* It can sometimes be tricky to set aside other aspects of our management role, but this is what we must sometimes do.
* Without trust, people will still answer our coaching questions but they will be superficial. Bland answers that take nothing forward are a waste of time.

TOP TIP
Try revealing some things you find difficult to your coachee. You can, for example, share that you're new to the coaching process and would appreciate their feedback afterwards.

Trust and other qualities

Trust in the process

* It is important that the people we coach understand the purpose of coaching.
* Remember that nobody likes to be singled out for 'special lessons'.
* It is vital that coaching is not used solely to address poor performance.
* Encourage even the highest performers to improve even more through coaching and share their success stories.

TOP TIP
Before beginning a detailed coaching conversation, try a little **'contracting'**. This means spending a few minutes outlining what coaching is and what it isn't, outlining how it will work, and giving the coachee an opportunity to raise any concerns.

Coaching qualities

I have asked people many times to list the qualities they'd look for in a coach. The top ten are:

1 good listening skills
2 trusting
3 trustworthy
4 empathetic
5 self-aware
6 positive
7 patient
8 non-judgemental
9 curious
10 good sense of humour.

Which of these do you need to develop?

Where does listening come in?

Effective listening

Listening with real focus is the most important element in establishing trust.

The **good** listener:

* rarely interrupts
* waits until the end then asks questions
* pays close attention
* verifies understanding by repetition/summaries
* gives feedback
* avoids arguing
* responds to ideas, not the person
* gets rid of distractions
* concentrates on words and feelings, stays on track.

The **poor** listener:

* always interrupts
* is impatient
* shows disinterest
* doesn't try to understand
* doesn't respond
* mentally prepares arguments to 'win'
* reacts to the person
* fidgets with pens, paper clips, etc.
* wanders off the subject.

In order to build a trusting coaching relationship…

Do:

✔ Consider having coaching conversations in a private space
✔ Let the coachee set the tone and pace
✔ Agree in advance how you will deal with any issues that might affect other people
✔ Decide between you how much note-taking is appropriate

Don't:

✘ Force people to be coached
✘ Have coaching conversations where you may be overheard
✘ Discuss the content of a coaching conversation with others
✘ Leave notes on the session or agreed actions where they might be seen by others

'You must trust and believe in people or life becomes impossible.'

Anton Chekhov

The three principles of coaching

Coaching is an ART

While this book has not been designed necessarily to be read cover to cover, the three previous chapters have covered the three key principles of effective coaching:

1 Awareness   2 Responsibility   3 Trust

This gives the acronym **ART**, which is a useful reminder that coaching people at work is not scientific. You and your people are complex human beings with a wide range of needs and feelings.

No book on coaching can cover every eventuality and circumstance.

Other chapters in this book set out in detail the models and frameworks to help you coach, **but without an appreciation of the importance of awareness, responsibility and trust, they will not work**.

CASE STUDY: Lexus

My firm once did some work with Lexus whose customers are typically high-powered, often wealthy individuals used to getting their own way and getting it quickly.

The customer relations department would have to respond to mistakes and complaints extremely fast so there was no time for complicated, lengthy referral procedures.

Instead, the senior managers coached the advisers and trusted them to do whatever was necessary – including financially – to keep the customer in the brand as far as was reasonably possible.

Feeling trusted to this extent, the advisers were actually very careful in how they spent the company's money and always made sure there was a sound business case for doing so.

6 Coaching to set aims

What do you want?

A wise man once said:

'If you don't know where you're going, you'll end up somewhere else.'

Every coaching model and approach suggests **some form of goal setting** as part of the coaching process.

Here we'll use the term 'aims' as a catch-all for terminology like goals, objectives, targets and a host of other workplace expressions used to capture the essence of where we're trying to get to with any given situation.

Every coaching model and approach suggests some form of goal setting as part of the coaching process

* Setting aims and goals provides **a sense of purpose**.
* Setting aims gives **a sense of direction**. People are able to more easily make the right choices; ones that are in line with their aims.
* Aims provide a series of **stepping stones** towards the bigger picture.
* Well-articulated aims provide an easy way to accurately **review progress**.
* Setting aims provides a vision or a picture of **what success will be like**.

A questioning framework

Introducing the coaching ARROW

We will also use this section to introduce an acronym – ARROW – to help us organize our questioning approach to coaching:

* **A**ims – what do you want?
* **R**eality – what's happening now?
* **R**eflection – how big is the gap?
* **O**ptions – what could you do?
* **W**ay forward – what will you do?

'A person who aims at nothing is sure to hit it.'

Anonymous

Dreams

Turning firstly then to aims:

* people need a variety of aims and there are **different sorts of aims**
* helping people become **focused on their aims** is an important part of successful coaching.

There also need to be dream-level aims – a big picture, **something inspiring and worthwhile**. For example, for a footballer this could be to win the World Cup; for a manager in a charity it may be to see a children's home being built.

TOP TIP
While we need dreams to provide inspiration, without taking some action they're pointless.

Effective goals

SMART goals

Following on from dreams, we need goals to provide a specification – to define what success will look like and the series of short-term achievements that will lead towards the dream.

For the footballer, these would be around defining when they want to make the team and the year of the tournament in which they want to play. The fundraising manager aiming to build a children's home will need goals around the amount of money needed and a start date for laying the foundations.

There are numerous goal-setting models around, but the following is the most well known:

* **S**pecific
* **M**easurable
* **A**chievable
* **R**ealistic
* **T**ime bound

PURE goals

The SMART model is so well known that perhaps people have stopped thinking about it properly and forget there are other things to consider in fully formulating a goal that is clear and drives people towards success.

For example, we should also consider:

* **P**ositive – goals around what's to be achieved rather than what's to be avoided
* **U**nderstandable – not too complex or unwieldy
* **R**elevant – where it's easy to see how they fit with a bigger picture
* **E**thical – goals that people feel are right and which don't conflict with their values

Too many models and acronyms risk putting the cart before the horse, but the point is that successful goal setting in a coaching conversation does need a little thought if the goal is going to drive the right behaviours.

From goals to processes

Negativity

* As outlined previously, goals are best stated in the **positive**. If we say to a child, 'Don't drop that glass', they tend to drop it.

* While language works in the negative, **the brain does not**. The child will first conceive dropping the glass and if feeling a little stressed will tend to do exactly that.

* Compare the effect of me saying to an assistant, 'Don't forget to post that proposal', with, 'Please ensure that the proposal is posted by 5 p.m.'.

Processes

* We need process aims to set out the steps and tasks that will **lead towards** the various goals which, in turn, are set against the dream.
* For the footballer these will include developing fitness and technique and the tactical awareness necessary to become a top player.
* For the fundraising manager it will include a range of activities around building networks, staging events, generating press interest, etc.

In summary, we need dreams to provide the **inspiration**, goals to provide the **specification**, and processes to provide the **mechanism**.

'A goal without a plan is just a wish.'

Larry Elder

Questions to set aims

Example questions

Here are some example questions **you can try**:

With regard to your situation…

1 What is the aim of this coaching conversation?
2 What are you trying to achieve long term?
3 How much control do you have over the outcome?
4 What is a short-term goal to achieve first?
5 When could you achieve that?
6 Is that short-term goal SMART, PURE, etc?
7 How will you measure your success?

and so on…

'A goal properly set is halfway reached.'

Abraham Lincoln

CASE STUDY: Aiming for a good degree

Alex dreamt of getting a good degree but she was beginning to feel it was beyond her reach. She had a 12,000-word dissertation to write which seemed an overwhelming amount of work in the two months she had left.

Through discussions with her coach, Alex realized there were three key sections in her dissertation; this meant 4,000 words per section. She then worked out each section could be divided into ten 400-word sections – introduction, summary and eight parts in between.

All of a sudden Alex was faced with simply a series of 400-word essays that would combine to make up the whole dissertation. She knew she could easily produce that every day for a month and that would then leave her another month for revisions and amendments.

7 Coaching to check reality

What's happening now?

In his recent book *The Grand Design*, renowned physicist Professor Stephen Hawking sets out the evidence that there is no truly objective reality; just the reality we each perceive as true for ourselves. Put more simply: there is no such thing as reality, there is simply **perception**.

This is a challenge in coaching, namely, we can never assume that our **coachee's perception** of situations is identical to ours. Where it is different we cannot assume that they are 'wrong' and we are 'right'.

We can never assume that our coachee's perception of situations is identical to ours

Therefore exploring perceptions and asking questions at the reality stage is a crucial part of effective coaching.

Do:

- ✔ Focus on what is actually happening
- ✔ Challenge without being confrontational
- ✔ Ask what evidence they have to support their view
- ✔ Recognize that an accurate view of reality must acknowledge what's going well

Don't:

- ✘ Merely exchange opinions
- ✘ Challenge their perceptions too soon
- ✘ Over-analyse
- ✘ Allow things to become downbeat

Exploring our perception

What do you see in Figure 7.1 – A B C or 12 13 14?

Figure 7.1: Visual puzzle

Now solve the puzzle on the opposite page…

Mum and Dad

Mum and Dad have spent their last few years aimlessly wandering around their home looking at four plain walls. On a rainy day, you will go and collect them. As you approach the premises you hear screaming coming from inside. You rush in to find, to your horror, Mum and Dad lying in a pool of water by a broken window, writhing in agony. Soon they are both dead, their unblinking eyes staring up at you. Their horribly mutilated bodies are surrounded by pieces of glass. The screaming has stopped, all is quiet now. The only sound you hear is the drip, drip, drip of a water tap. Suddenly, a sound by the open door makes you spin round – you catch a brief glimpse of a male in a wet, black coat creeping slowly out of the front door.

Take a few moments to review the information provided and work out what has happened. Read on for an explanation…

Interpreting what we see

We supply our own interpretation of things and our perception is not always the same as another's. It is very easy to get stuck in a revolving argument around who is 'wrong' and who is 'right'.

In coaching this is unhelpful. We should instead remain curious and ask our coachees to talk more about how they reach their conclusions.

Let's try another test. How many triangles can you see in Figure 7.2?

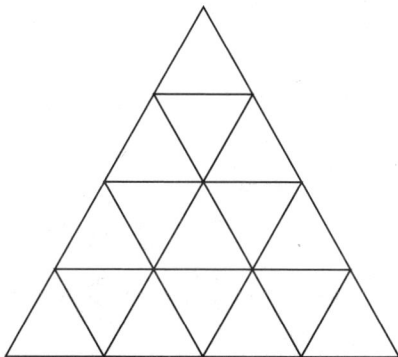

Figure 7.2: Pyramid puzzle

There are, in fact, 27. Keep looking until you can see them all.

Questions to explore reality

We do not see everything right away and so the reality stage is not one I would ever recommend rushing.

It is very important to **allow the other person** to get their perception of reality as clear and accurate as possible because we make our decisions based on our perception of reality.

> **'Reality is merely an illusion, albeit a very persistent one.'**
>
> Albert Einstein

Example questions

Here are some example questions **you can try**:

With regard to your situation…

1 What is happening now?
2 How much or how often is that happening?
3 Who is involved?
4 How does this situation affect you and others?
5 What have you done about this so far?
6 What results did that produce?

and so on…

Do you make assumptions?

Here are the answers and explanation to that puzzle about Mum and Dad I set you earlier in this chapter:

A mystery solved...

Mum and Dad are goldfish for sale in a local pet shop. You are going to buy them. A cat got in via a broken window, scared a parrot and proceeded to try to fish Mum and Dad out of their tank. In doing so the tank was knocked to the floor and smashed – water and glass going everywhere. You disturb the cat as he is preparing to eat the fish. He quickly hides and then slowly starts to make his escape. While making a getaway, the cat makes a slight noise and you see him creeping out of the door.

This illustrates the danger of making assumptions.

CASE STUDY: Dealing with stress

Jo worked as an administration assistant in a large HR department. She found her job very difficult and often complained of feeling pretty stressed.

Her boss and colleagues responded with comments like 'Stress? She doesn't have the first idea' and 'She should try my job for a day, that'll teach her about stress'. Quite soon, Jo was on sick leave – in the end for a total of six months – and being treated for depression.

Had her firm recognized that to Jo her situation really was stressful – even though it did not seem so to others – they could have been saved an awful lot of time and money. More importantly, Jo could have been helped much sooner.

8 Coaching for reflection

Time to think...

If you're reading this book straight through, cover to cover, please stop and go and do something else while you think about what you've read.

Welcome back! How did that feel?

It's likely you ignored the instruction completely or became impatient and returned to the book quickly because – I hear you say – we're busy and we **don't have time to think!** Coaching is about legitimately making time in our working lives for a good, hard think.

Coaching is about legitimately making time in our working lives for a good, hard think

* When was the last time – during work – that you kicked back and just spent some time thinking?
* Most people think this would be a sure recipe for getting fired!
* We've become so busy 'doing' we've lost sight of the fact – since all our actions are preceded by thought – that **higher-quality thinking leads to better-quality decisions and actions**.
* Coaching someone offers them an opportunity to do their very best thinking.
* Reflecting and thinking are crucial elements of good coaching before, during and after the actual coaching conversation.
* R for reflection is conveniently located in the middle of the ARROW sequence but we will consider the wider value of reflection here.

A pause for reflection

Reflection for the coach

Taking a pause for reflection within a coaching conversation provides the coach with an opportunity to think, too.

Tim Gallwey's Transpose tool recommends putting ourselves in the coachee's shoes and considering three key questions:

1 What am I thinking?
2 What am I feeling?
3 What do I want?

…the answers to which help shape the direction of the conversation.

Reflection for the coachee

Creating a definite time for reflection within the ARROW sequence leads to a better outcome. With aims and reality discussed, the coachee can consider how big a task they have in bridging the gap.

Perhaps their aims may look a bit over-optimistic on reflection. Perhaps they seem a bit modest in truth and on reflection they could be more stretching. Perhaps they come to realize they don't really have a firm grip on the current reality. It might be that they haven't fully considered all points of view or taken time to consider how other people are affected by what's going on.

Either way, before considering options for what could be done or deciding what actually to do, time for reflection is crucial.

Finding a blockage

Reflecting between coaching sessions

Of course, thinking and learning go on between coaching conversations as well as during. In fact, it's a bit like a sandwich:

* the coaching is the bread, the actions are the filling
* the real learning takes place as we take action on the things we've thought about.

Where's the blockage?

Sometimes our coachees get stuck and a coaching conversation grinds to a halt. It can be useful to reflect on where the blockage might be:

* **Head** – they still don't quite understand. Perhaps the situation is very messy and complicated and despite a thorough coaching conversation some things remain unclear or confusing.
* **Heart** – they don't believe in what's being explored. Perhaps it's an age-old or ongoing problem and absolutely everything that could be tried has already been tried. Some action steps are emerging but they were tried last year and didn't work then so the coachee doesn't think they would work now.
* **Guts** – they lack the courage to take action. What if the aim is to have a fulfilling job but the reality suggests that will never be possible in their current role or even in their current organization? Perhaps what's truly needed is a career change, but what are the chances of finding the right job and what about paying the bills in the meantime?

Questions for reflection

Example questions

Here are some example questions **you can try**:

With regard to your situation…

1. How big is the gap between aims and reality?
2. How realistic are your aims?
3. How certain are you about the reality of the situation?
4. How could you find out more?
5. What assumptions are you making?
6. Have you been totally honest with yourself?
7. What's really going on?

and so on…

Some of these questions are worth looking at in more detail…

For instance, **what assumptions are you making?**

* People have a tendency to hear what they want to hear and see what they want to see.
* Part of reflection is to consider whether people are working with known facts or possibly **false assumptions**.
* Remember the acronym, ASSUME – 'Assume makes an ASS out of U (you) and ME'.

TOP TIP
In order to create a pause for yourself while coaching, consider asking 'What else?' as a follow-up to any other coaching question.

A need for honesty

And **are you being totally honest with yourself?**

* Unless your people do not trust you at all, it is unlikely they will blatantly lie in answering your coaching questions.
* However, they may lie to themselves, perhaps even unconsciously, to avoid confronting an uncomfortable truth.
* This question allows such things to rise to the surface and then we can coach around them.

94

> **'And time for reflection with colleagues is for me a lifesaver; it is not just a nice thing to do if you have the time. It is the only way you can survive.'**
>
> Margaret J. Wheatley

CASE STUDY: Coaching boosts career

Zane was being coached on his tendency towards self-sabotage. He was a gifted web designer and was highly sought after.

However, when big contracts came his way he would often procrastinate and fail to follow up and eventually the contract would go to another designer. His coach asked: 'What's really going on?'

It emerged that Zane believed that if he were really successful, it would make him very different to his friends and family. He worried that his success might alienate them and he would end up on his own.

Of course, once this was out in the open, it was easy for Zane and his coach to plot ways of avoiding this outcome without having to forgo his chances of success.

9 Coaching to generate options

What could you do?

Coaching is an especially useful tool when it comes to **helping people think creatively**. Whether we are using coaching to develop a skill or solve a problem it is necessary for our coachees to explore new ways of moving forward.

No doubt we've all been encouraged to **'think outside the box'**, but what exactly does this mean and how might it be different to thinking 'inside the box'?

It is necessary for our coachees to explore new ways of moving forward
....

The problem is that our **thinking gets stuck**:

* we pursue the same old tired ideas in the hope they may finally work
* this is compounded if, sometimes, these ideas do work a little
* as the old saying goes, **'even a stopped clock is right twice a day'**, which means that we stick with old methods because they occasionally bring a result.

However, we can use coaching questions to get people unstuck; to tap into their creative juices and generate some energy by **breathing new life into old problems**.

What if...?

Break assumptions

The danger of working on assumptions is covered in the previous chapter on coaching for reflection. Coaching to generate options requires us as coaches to **challenge and break assumptions**.

TOP TIP
Try challenging assumptions by asking: 'How do you know that?' or 'What's your evidence?'

Asking 'What if…' is a great way to challenge assumptions and get people thinking ahead creatively.

Example questions

Here are some example questions **you can try**:

1 What if you had more time?
2 What if you were the boss?
3 What if you had more budget?
4 What if that obstacle were not there?
5 What if you were guaranteed to succeed?

and so on…

How to keep the ideas flowing

Write everything down

* I like to coach with a flipchart pad and a load of pens nearby.
* It's important at this stage to make sure ideas don't get lost.
* It can be useful for the coach to do the writing, leaving the coachee free to keep thinking creatively.

Reserve judgement

* Judging and evaluating ideas too soon stops the flow and discourages further contributions.
* Being too critical saps confidence and the willingness to come up with more ideas.
* In a team coaching situation this can put off everyone else, too.

'One cool judgement is worth a thousand hasty counsels. The thing to do is to supply light and not heat.'
Woodrow T. Wilson

Weighing up the options

Would you like another idea?

* Sometimes as a coach you will have an idea that you'd love to offer, but it is wise to hold back.
* If the coachee 'owns' the idea, they are more likely to work to make it succeed.
* If you give them the solution, they have a ready-made excuse if it doesn't immediately succeed.

Stopping at the first option

We are probably coaching against a timescale and it is very tempting to move on as soon as a half-decent idea has emerged. However, this is unlikely to be as useful and imaginative as others that could be generated with a little more work.

Stopping at the 'right' option

Some coaches work at the options stage until the coachee eventually comes up with what the coach thinks they should do!

Questions to generate options

Example questions

Here are some example questions **you can try**:

With regard to your situation…

1 What could you do?
2 What else could you try?
3 And what else?
4 What if you had more/less…?
5 Would you like another suggestion?
6 What are the costs and benefits of each option?

and so on…

'Significant problems we have cannot be solved at the same level of thinking with which we created them.'

Albert Einstein

CASE STUDY: Following one's heart

When I first set up my consultancy I struggled to bring in enough clients by myself to grow the business. My coach helped me generate some options and I was considering creating a mailshot, hiring a telesales agency and various other conventional marketing ideas.

Then my coach asked me a killer options question: 'What would you do if you knew you couldn't fail.'

'I would hire a salesperson,' I replied instantly, 'I've thought about it before, but it's a big commitment and I'm frightened that it might not work out.'

The coaching then turned to how I could make the idea work as it was clearly what I truly wanted to do. Fear was driving me towards the other, safer options but my heart wasn't in them.

10 Coaching to gain commitment to the way forward

What are you going to do?

One of the biggest time wasters in organizations is the 'cosy chat' with **no specific actions agreed**.

As coaches we must help people determine what they are actually going to do and which of their options they are willing to put into practice.

One of the biggest time wasters in organizations is the 'cosy chat' with no specific actions agreed

••

* We can help people commit to the way forward by summarizing available options and helping the coachee **make a choice**.
* They may **choose one or several options** or a blend of the various alternatives.
* We should also check that a chosen action will take them **towards their aims**.
* Any support that is needed can be discussed and arranged.

Be firm but fair

The most difficult question is: when? With effective coaching – that generates responsibility in the coachee – agreeing a time frame should be quite straightforward.

However, it can be quite **tough for people to make a firm commitment**, so we should be careful not to coach in an aggressive way.

The coach's job is to remove the risk of the coachee letting themselves down by not following through.

Beware of backflow – this is a tendency to try to shift the problem back to the manager:

* emphasize the 'you' in the coaching questions, 'What are *you* going to do?', 'When are *you* going to do it?', etc.
* by all means ask 'What do you need me to do?' but make sure that you are supporting the coachee in taking action, not the other way round.

TOP TIP
Make a date to follow up with your coachee. It is much more likely they will follow through if they know you will be meeting them again to discuss progress.

Encouraging people to change

Overcome resistance

* Human beings are creatures of habit and we seem to prefer the status quo, hence expressions like **'better the devil you know'**.
* Only when the need to change is recognized as being greater than the reluctance to do so will the **balance tip in favour of taking action**.

Human beings are creatures of habit and we seem to prefer the status quo...

Rate commitment

* A great question to ask at this stage is, 'How willing are you to take this agreed action?' or something along those lines.
* I like to get people to quantify their answer using a 1–10 scale.
* While some people are uncomfortable with this, and find it a bit pushy, it's all about making sure that people can be successful and feel solely **responsible for their success**.
* This is a sure-fire recipe for ongoing confidence and performance.

'The way to get started is to quit talking and begin doing.'
Walt Disney

Questions for the way forward

Challenge commitment

What if people tell us they're only 5, 6, or 7 out of 10 committed to taking the action they've indentified?

Recognize that they aren't going to do it! Either coach for further commitment or **cross it off the list** and go back to the options.

> **TOP TIP**
> To reveal where the reluctance lies, try asking: 'What stops it being 10?' or 'What would have to change to make it 10?'

Example questions

Here are some more example questions **you can try**:

With regard to your situation…

1 What are you going to do?
2 When are you going to do it?
3 Who needs to know?
4 What support do you need?
5 How will you get that support?
6 Can you rate on a 1–10 scale your willingness to take this action?

and so on…

A reward for your commitment

Now just before I give you a final case study to consider, let me say that I hope you've enjoyed this short guide to the skill and art of coaching. Even though the Bullet Guide series has been designed to be quick and easy to digest, finding the time to read and think about the material requires a degree of commitment.

I have therefore produced an extra chapter called 'Coaching in teams' exclusively for readers of this book. You can download it by visiting www.mattsomers.com/extrachapter

NB: You will be asked to enter some information found in the book as proof that you have a copy.

I wish you every success with your coaching.

CASE STUDY: A tale of two start-ups

Victoria and Geri set up their coaching practices on the same day. Victoria began by studiously designing her logo and seeking quotes from printers for her business cards and compliment slips. Geri began by coaching her neighbour's daughter in exam technique in exchange for a testimonial she could upload to her website.

Victoria gave design briefs to three different web development agencies. She chose a firm that was able to set out her coaching certificates as little animations that flashed across the screen. Geri persuaded a top web designer to throw up a quick page that set out the results she could guarantee to achieve. She coached the designer in return and received a great testimonial to use.

Geri has a thriving practice and a growing client list. Victoria is considering undertaking some further coaching skills training.

Further reading

Gallwey, W. Timothy, *The Inner Game of Tennis* (Random House, 1997)

Gallwey, W. Timothy, *The Inner Game of Work* (Random House, 2001)

Kline, Nancy, *Time to Think: Listening to Ignite the Human Mind* (Cassell, 1999)

Pink, Daniel H., *Drive: The Surprising Truth About What Motivates Us* (Canongate Books, 2011)

Somers, Matt, *Coaching at Work* (John Wiley & Sons, 2006)

Whitmore, John, *Coaching for Performance* (Nicholas Brealey Publishing, 2009)